Cora Randall Fabbri

Lyrics

Cora Randall Fabbri

Lyrics

ISBN/EAN: 9783743328334

Manufactured in Europe, USA, Canada, Australia, Japa

Cover: Foto ©ninafisch / pixelio.de

Manufactured and distributed by brebook publishing software
(www.brebook.com)

Cora Randall Fabbri

Lyrics

LYRICS

BY

CORA FABBRI

MDCC CXCII
NEW YORK

HARPER & BROTHERS

CONTENTS

THE SPIRIT OF SPRING

From the perilous, pale, silent snows,
Like a dream from the Eastern-night's loom;
Like a star from the depth of the gloom,
Like a hope from the door of the tomb
     I arise;
Till a song blossoms out from the still,
And the lights that are flecking the hill
Gather strength, overflow, and then fill
     All the skies.

The clouds, when I touch them, divide,
And fall in a flutter of snow
That the tangled green vines catch below,
And the golden sun-swords prick and glow
     Where they close.
I scatter dew-pearls that intwine
As they fall where the limpid lights shine,
Till the flake in the leaf-tangled vine
     Is a rose.

1

I breathe in a half-open leaf
All the secrets that sigh through the seas,
Through the sweeps of the flowering leas,
Through the dew-dusted wings of the breeze
   All unheard;
Till the life which my breath can endow
Trembles out of a sudden—and now
The half-open leaf on the bough
   Is a bird.

The naiads asleep in a cloud
Fleet down by their star-strewn stair
To the calm whisp'ring water, and there
They wind the wan buds in their hair
   One by one.
The prints of their rosy feet dwell
On the edge of the pale lily-bell,
And the lizard creeps out from his cell
   To the sun.

Like a song dawning out of a hush,
With the sound of soft wind in my hair,
And the breath of new buds on the air,
And a vision of birds everywhere
   On the wing,

I have come, with a gift of fair hours,
With the singing of birds in new bowers.
I am queen of the stars and the flowers—
      I am Spring!

MOON-SHADOWS

A SONNET

I LEANED out from my window yesternight,
And saw the whole sky luminous and pale
From the moon, wrapt in a cloud's filmy veil,
As when one shades a candle out of sight
Behind the hollowed palm, letting the light
Fall o'er the shadowed room. Across each vale
The wind on tiptoe sped and shook the frail,
Top branches of the pine - tree in its flight.

Lady, thine eyes' eclipse hath drawn the rare
White moon of joy behind a cloud, and stole
Its star-tide ; yet thy memory is there
To shed its soft light where the shadows roll.
I lean out from the window of my soul,
And see my whole sky luminous and fair.

WOMAN'S WAY

AYE, that's our woman's way. We lean our faith
Upon one thing, which often proves too weak
And fails us. We are given overmuch
To trust our heart—whole heart—into one hand,
Which, growing weary, lets it drop, perhaps,
And then we pick it up and weep to find
That it is broken.
          Were I only strong
(Which is to say, no woman), I would strip
From out my heart and out my reeling brain
The tortuous thought of him who proved so false,
As I have stript my finger of the ring
That means no more now than a band of gold.
If I were strong, I'd never go out at eve,
When all the fire-flies, like sparks of light
Dropped from the mystic burning stars, are out
And flitting low, and playing hide-and-seek
With pretty buds, and ev'ry breeze let loose
Is making havoc of the golden wheat;

I'd never go with hurried, stealthy tread
To where we stood together at the gate
One time—and not so very long ago—
To stand alone now—aye, that's sad—at least
It's sad to dream on the Impossible;
To stand and think with mournful eyes and lips,
More des'late, sure, than wet and easeful tears,
Upon the Past. Why, sometimes, I confess
The life-blood rushes backward on my heart,
As if to hush its throbbing—just because
I think I hear a step that sounds like his.
Oh yes! the best of us are only weak!

If I were strong, I'd brand his image, "false,"
And stamp it into powder 'neath my feet.
Instead, I've got it still—I've laid it by
With all his letters.
                    On drear winter nights,
When I am sitting by my lonely hearth,
I count them over, and I think how once
He sat so near me on that other chair
(Which I have left there still—because I'm weak)—
So near, our hands met. Just to break the still
That grows so mournful, I can hear my tears;
In low half-whispers I repeat sometimes

The sweet, fond love-names ever on our lips—
Elsewise I have forgotten how they sound.

If I were strong, and he should come to-night
And stand before me on the threshold there
With out-stretched hands, the love-light in his eyes
(That once I deemed unquenchable) relit;
The half smile on his lips I know so well—
If peradventure he should come (and I
Were strong, you understand), I'd fling my scorn
Into his face, and bid him go, and cry,
"I have forgot you and those blissful days—
I've bound my heart up—far off from your reach,
And all your love could never touch it now"...
If I were strong! ...

      ... I think if he should come
And stand upon the threshold there some day,
And whisper once, "My wife"—no other word—
I think I'd say, "Come in; I've kept your place."

Well, I'm a woman—and we're very weak ...

LADYE MAUDE

ADOWN the dim-lit gallery I stept;
  My foot awoke the echoes slumb'ring there,
  A sunbeam fell with light subdued and fair
Upon the pictured forms of those who slept,

Gilding the portraits dim upon the wall,
  Of stately dames and stalwart warriors bold;
  Of virgins fair, with eyes both bright and cold,
And each has answered Death's imperial call.

An ancient portrait, mellowed by the gloom,
  A pair of smiling lips, and cold, still face.
  Time's heedless hand had hastened to erase
The name below. The rest was in the tomb.

Musing, I paused before one form, amid
  The shadows dense and dark. Across the face
  A filmy web was stretched; each pictured grace
By dust of gath'ring years was wellnigh hid.

I swept the dust away with reverent touch,
  And gazed upon the face in dim surprise.
  A little maid demure, with large, sad eyes,
Looked startled back at me, as though o'ermuch

My gaze had ventured on her dreams. The lips
  Were wistful, and the face was over-grave
  For one so young. The light crept on and gave
A mellowed radiance. Gold the sunbeam slips

From cheeks to lips, from lips to shoulders white,
  The pearl-bound throat bore high with stately grace
  The small, proud head and young, pure, flower-
    like face ;
Her large-eyed gaze met mine across the light.

And underneath the pictured form was this:
  "The Ladye Maude, born 1652,
  Died 1674." So young! The rue
Was greater mingled in those years than bliss.

Musing, I gazed through retrospection's veil
  Into those wistful eyes, and read therein
  The tale I knew so well of what had been.
Oh, little Ladye Maude, so sad a tale !
  2

Here, while the dusk comes on, and in the gloom,
  List to the story, of those few short years;
  List to the mournful tale and let your tears
Drop down, drop down, for her within the tomb:

    In the garden fair with Spring,
      Where the stately lilies grow,
    Where the green-leafed tree-tops swing,
      Tipped with blossoms as with snow,
    There the Ladye Maude did tread,
    Fairer than the roses red,
    Brighter than the sun o'erhead.

    In her kirtle purely white,
      And her hood of silver sheen,
    With her face demurely bright,
      Oft she stood beneath the green
    By the ivied castle gate;
    There she used to stand and wait
    Where the sunbeams lingered late.

    Wait till in the distance far
      She could faintly see her love.
    With the birth of twilight's star,
      With the first gray shades above,

He would come to where she stood
Waiting by the leafy wood,
Perfect in her womanhood.

Then she welcomed her true knight,
  Blissful shining in her face ;
And the blossoms fell down white,
  Carpeting their trysting-place,
Happy in their perfect love ;
Only did the nested dove
Break the twilight's still above.

Ladye Maude, O Ladye Maude !
  Fell a sadness on thine heart?
Did the shadow of the sword
  That would cleft ye two apart
Strike betwixt thy joy and his—
Steal the sweetness from thy bliss,
And the warmness from his kiss ?

Ere the blossoms white were dead,
  War-red blood within his hand,
Dearth and mis'ry in his tread,
  Awful swept throughout the land.

Now her true, brave knight was gone,
And the Ladye Maude each morn
In her turret sat forlorn.

Every night beside the gate
   That had been their trysting-spot
Stood the Ladye desolate,
   For his gallant steed came not.
To the war her knight was fled,
Fighting now among the dead,
With his sword all bloody red.

Still the weary time sped on;
   Each day brought its deeper pain,
Woke her tears and killed her song;
   For her knight came not again,
And no tidings stilled the woe
That her heart began to know,
And that grew and still did grow.

Every night beside the gate,
   Desolate, alone, she stood.
Patiently she learned to wait;
   With her strength of womanhood—

Trembling strength—she bravely fought
'Gainst the pain his absence wrought,
Strove to hold her fears for naught.

But the flame of hope soon died,
  And she beat her hands in woe;
"To the battle-field," she cried,
  "Where my knight is, I must go!
I will succor bring with speed,
I will find him in his need;
Straightway bring my gallant steed."

Ere the golden morning broke
  She had donned her male attire,
And before the sun awoke,
  Lighting up the distant spire,
She was speeding on her way,
In the dawn-light, dim and gray,
Where the battle meadow lay.

On and on she swifter sped,
  Urging still her panting steed,
And the sky grew rosy red . . .
  "I will find him in his need.

Jesus," did the Ladye say,
"Guard me, guide me, smooth my way
Straight into the battle fray."

Straight into the battle-field
  Where the dead lay, far and wide,
Gallant knights who once did wield
  Sword and lances side by side.
Ah! she shuddered at the sight
Of the blood so red and bright,
And she called to her dear knight.

There she saw him, far away,
  Fighting as the heroes fought.
And she swept amid the fray
  Nearer to the one she sought.
Nearer to her love she came,
Then she called aloud his name :
Loudly, with no thought of shame.

All the warriors round her saw
  But a fragile, fearless boy,
Sweeping onward evermore,
  With a look of wondrous joy.

Saw they not Death's missiles fly,
Heard they not the ringing cry,
Nor did see her fall and die.

But the stalwart knight behind,
　Whom her form had shielded well,
Saw her in a glory shrined
　As she turned, and smiled, and fell.
Swift he dropped his bloody sword,
And he cried aloud on God,
For he knew his Ladye Maude.

*　　*　　*　　*　　*　　*

Quiet lay the battle-field,
　Ghastly underneath the moon ;
Every warrior who did wield
　His good sword, or late or soon,
Lay upon the meadow dead,
Stiff, upon his last hard bed ;
Calm the stars looked down o'erhead.

Pale the moon rose, full and round,
　Liquid bright behind the hill ;
And it shone upon the ground
　Where two dead lay, cold and still ;

Wrapt in one long, close embrace,
Heart to heart, and face to face,
Battle-field their trysting-place.

He the stalwart warrior died
   For his country — it was well;
But the woman at his side,
   For her love's dear sake she fell.
Red between them lies his sword,
Ne'er to part them, now with God,
Happy now, O Ladye Maude!

AN OLD MAID

GRAY hair softly, smoothly parting
  O'er a brow where sorrow lies ;
Eyes pathetic in their sadness,
Eyes that shame you from your gladness,
  Tender, honest, wistful eyes ;
  And two lips where smiles are rarer than the
    sudden, fleeting sighs.

Two worn hands forever busy,
  Toiling all the morning long,
When glad human souls are smiling
Underneath the sunshine, whiling
  Idle hours with their song ;
  And no conscience voice is calling, telling them
    that they are wrong.

Thus I see her ever sitting
  Through the morn, and when the night
3

O'er the earth and sea is breaking,
When the myriad stars are waking,
  Heaving, throbbing into sight,
    And when other mortals wander hand in hand
    beneath the light.

Peradventure when the silence
  Hath grown stronger, and the gloom
Deepens into purple splendor ;
When the moon-queen's crescent slender
  O'er the hill begins to loom—
    Then her griefs, through daytime maskèd, darker,
    drearer shapes assume.

Then her heartache 'gins to waken,
  For she is so lone !—so lone !—
Ah ! poor lips that lack the clinging
Of warm kisses, and the ringing
  Of child laughter is unknown
    To this woman sitting silent when the eve to
    night hath grown.

Where she sitteth 'tis most quiet,
  No small print of feet is there ;

No dropped toy child hands have broken ;
No love speeches, no love token,
　　No glad laughter anywhere.
　　Ah, poor heart, ne'er stirred to throbbing by a
　　footstep on the stair !

Do you say, you happy mothers
　　With your children at your side,
That this woman's life is wasted
Just because she has not tasted
　　Of Love's cup? Because the tide
　　Of her mother-love strikes inward and is left
　　unsatisfied?

Wasted ? Yes, this heart, this woman
　　Makes no mortal's Paradise.
At her leaving none grow sadder,
And no tender soul is gladder
　　For the brightening of her eyes.
　　What o'er-watchful heart is burdened for the
　　falling of her sighs?

Wasted ? Yes, the tender romance
　　Of her youthful days is dead ;

Evermore the sweet tale ended,
Where such joy and grief were blended ;
  Love from out her life hath fled.
  But "Be all the mourners blessèd," Jesus Christ
  divinely said.

And this woman, toiling, toiling,
  With that sorrow in her eyes,
Walks her path in unrepining,
Furthest from the intertwining
  Light of sunshine. All her skies
  Lower darkly ; smiles are rarer to her lips than
  mournful sighs.

Yet she bears her cross most bravely,
  Helping those who help may need.
Wasted ? Nay, this life is duly
Beauteous, and her record truly
  Is most noble, blest indeed ;
  Such a record, oh, you mothers, as the angels
  love to read.

SONG

If the bird
Had no list'ner, wrapt, adoring;
If its song in joyous soaring
    Fell upon the air unheard;
If no flower-lips, entrancèd
Where the golden sunbeam glancèd,
Drank the song the bird was flinging,
What would be the use of singing?

If the flower,
Lifting up its petaled crown
Where the sun comes filt'ring down,
    Never felt the summer shower;
If no busy, vagrant bees
Came to woo it with the breeze;
If no golden light was flooding,
What would be the use of budding?

If the heart
Never felt the quick pulsation,
Never knew the sweet elation
    That of faithful love is part;
If lips lacked the warmth of kissing;
If the tender words were missing
That true hearts delight in giving,
What would be the use of living?

THE POET

DOES the poet understand what the nightingale
   at night
                  Sweetly sings ?
Pouring out her secret heart to the pure and pale
   moonlight ?
Does he understand the meaning of the singing
                  That is ringing
                  Ev'rywhere
                  On the air ?

Does the poet comprehend what the pearl pink-
   linèd shell
                  Murmurs faint ?
Does it tell him all the secrets that the foam-
   touched wavelets tell,
As they fling their arms caressing on the gleaming,

Golden, beaming,
Shell-strewn floor
Of the shore?

Does the poet hear the secrets of the fair - lipped
    flowers sweet?
What they say
To each other? Does he listen while we tread
    them 'neath our feet,
Just to hear the fragrant whisper — catch the
    meaning
Of the leaning
Roses red
In their bed?

Does the poet hear the song through the music of
    the stream
Fresh and clear,
As it ripples, dances on — on to meet the gold
    sunbeam,
Which is waiting 'mid the shadows that are
    lying
In the sighing
Weeping willow
Near the billow?

Tell us, poet, are you gifted that these things you
    understand,
                And can read
Nature's poems in the book she holds within her
    hand?
And for us who cannot open it or read it
                You repeat it,
                That we know it?
                Do you, poet?

4

OLD LETTERS

Turn the light low, let the moonbeams stray
Through the window open wide,
And now leave me quite alone,
With these letters by my side,

In the gloaming gray and dim,
With the birds' sweet good-night hymn
Floating from the distance in.

All alone and yet not lonely,
For what throngs of mem'ries come
When I lift these letters worn,
Old and yellow, one by one.

Loose tied with a ribbon blue
Of a tender, faded hue;
Signed alone: "Your sweetheart true."

In among the pages thin,
Heart's-ease that of old she wore;

They cannot cure my heartache now,,
As they used to once before;

As they used to long ago,
In those sweet old times, ah, no!
For they tell me but of woe.

In among these records fair
A sweet pictured face I see;
That face graven on my heart,
As it evermore will be.

Dainty head of golden hair,
Large blue eyes so sweet and fair,
Blue as hearts of violets rare.

Just the same that long ago
With that laughing, 'witching face,
Stole my heart, and left me glad
For a bright, brief summer space.

Oh, those happy, joyous hours
Passed among the dewy flowers
In the sunlit, scented bowers!

Then my cup of joy seemed full,
And it grew more so each day;
Till at last it overflowed,
Ran in sparkling drops away;

Left me sad and quite forlorn,
With a love that I must mourn,
With a bliss all past and gone.

A ring sent back—a lock of hair,
A letter, too—that we must part,
A few short words so coldly writ,
But ah, that letter broke my heart.

She knew I'd "see 'twere for the best,"
"We could be friends" (what words of jest!)
"Esteem," and—but you know the rest.

I cried to God, then, in my pain,
I could not live with this great loss;
But He taught me how instead
I must live and bear my cross.

So sped on year after year,
Life went all blank and drear,
Till the past seemed one dream fair.

Though her heart was faithless, I
Ne'er have loved her less, ah, no!
Some souls drink their cup of bliss
In one draught—with me 'twas so.

In that happy summer-time,
In those days all gold sunshine,
I had drunk and finished mine.

Now all is a dream long past;
Only as a memory here
Those few letters yellow lie,
Older, dimmer year by year.

And my heartache, as I lean
O'er these records, grows more keen
Thinking of what might have been.

God forgive me, He knows best;
'Tis His hand that sends all pain.
I have lived my sweet past o'er,
Sweet and bitter, once again.

Back I lay these letters few,
But I tie my heart up, too,
With this faded ribbon blue.

IF

If I were a bird
I would sing all day;
I would sing of you
To the dropping dew,
To the heaven's blue,
All the praise I knew,
Till the whole world heard—
If I were a bird.

If I were a flower—
Say a daisy small—
I would kiss your feet
When I saw you fleet
Pass me by, O sweet!
I would murmur "Dear"
All the summer hour—
If I were a flower.

If I were the wind—
Say a summer breeze—

I'd be bolder, dear:
I would kiss your ear,
I would touch your hair,
Catch a flying lock,
All its bands unbind—
If I were the wind.

If I were the rose,
Growing frail and white,
Near your window-sill,
I would climb until
I had reached it; still
I would climb and peep
Till the evening's close—
If I were a rose.

And if I were you .
I would act the same;
Only, did I see
Some one loving me
Standing near, I'd be
Just a trifle kind;
I would drop a few
Smiles, if I were you.

MEMORIA IN ETERNA

BENEATH the pale skies, dreaming
  Vague dreams of stars and night;
Across the small lake gleaming
  With last long rays of light—
My boat went speeding faster
Than the brown bird that passed her—
My boat went speeding faster
  Than the swift swallow's flight.

Across the gray lake floating—
  O Heart, have you forgot
That spot beneath the willows
  Which was our trysting - spot?
Two feet that came to meet me,
Two hands out-stretched to greet me,
Low whispers to repeat me
  Words cherished, unforgot.

The tangled vines held roses—
  Pale buds with folded leaf—

Set deep in thorns, like pleasures
  Born from a bed of grief,
And slender boughs held showers
Of snow from Winter hours,
Which Spring's breath kissed to flowers,
  As fleeting snowflakes brief.

O Heart, do you remember
  How close the violets grew?
How drooping willows touched us,
  And gold sun-swords pierced through?
I talked, as men do ever,
Of loves that falter never,
Of lives no hand can sever,
  Of hearts forever true.

I talked, as men do ever,
  Of all that was to be.
God filled my folded flowers
  With thorns I could not see.
Dear as a cherished token,
Fleet as a love-word spoken,
My dreams lie shattered, broken,
  In Death's eternal sea. . . .

3

Beneath the pale skies fading
　To mournful twilight gray,
My little boat goes floating,
　Alas! the same old way.
Only the gay birds fleeting,
And whisp'ring breezes meeting,
And winds and waters greeting,
　Have left me sad to-day.

Our trysting-spot is empty
　Under the willow-tree;
No tender blue eyes watch me,
　No dear lips smile at me;
And as the breeze goes sighing,
The mellow sunlight, dying,
Falls on a small grave lying
　Beneath a cypress-tree.

Dumb lips that will not answer,
　Blue eyes fast shut in sleep;
And if I left her, certes,
　She would not even weep.
The dreams of days departed
Have faded whence they started,
And I stand broken-hearted—
　Her dear lips smile in sleep.

I am weary of all life's pleasures
   For one lost pleasure's sake.
Pale buds of dead desire,
   Sharp thorns that dead flow'rs make, .
Have strewn my life with sorrow ;
To-morrow and to-morrow
Their sad-eyed grief will borrow
   For one dead maiden's sake.

Each day my boat goes thither,
   Where flowers are blowing yet,
Where suns will shine and shimmer,
   Although my eyes are wet.
My life is all November—
Bleak skies of chill December. . . .
O Heart, must thou remember ?
   'Twere better to forget.

WITH THE LINNETS

I AM lying in the grasses
   Underneath the cooling trees;
Overhead the linnet passes,
   Drifting on a summer breeze.
Hardly singing, for the silence
   Sweeter is than any song,
Like a dream of unfound islands
   Where white Peace reigns all day long.

Yes, the place so very still is
   That the dew one almost hears
Dropping softly in the lilies—
   Fleet, like little children's tears.
I forget, among the grasses—
   Ah, so easy thus to do!—
That this summer sweetness passes,
   And this heart-peace passes too.

Birds, I watch you in the shadows,
   And I see you fleeting by,

Springing from the sweet green meadows
Till you find the sweeter sky.
Had I wings, O linnet yonder,
Like your fleet brown wings unfurled,
I would rise with you, and wander
Till I had forgot the world.

Fleet across the hill-sides peaceful,
With a song for interlude,
Rest, with brown wings closed and easeful,
In some leafy solitude.
With no fear of any sorrow
Brooding through a moonless night,
With no thought of any morrow
That will mar to-day's delight.

So, forget the world men live in,
(And I lived in yesterday!)
Weary men that doubt of heaven,
Since God will not hear them pray.
Evil men, in all succeeding,
Since their hands are full of gold;
Hungry men, that none are heeding,
Though they stand out in the cold.

I would soar so near to heaven,
   I would doubt that such things are;
And the solemn church-yard even
   Would not grieve me from afar;
I would see it through Spring flowers,
   With the joy that flowers bring,
And between the twilight hours
   Pause above some grave to sing. . . .

Oh, you happy birds, fly onward,
   But I cannot follow yet;
Only will my dreams fly sunward,
   And forget what you forget.
Only, where this place so still is,
   I can lie among the grass,
Thinking, with the happy lilies,
   That this peace will never pass.

DIED YOUNG

AND she is sleeping now without a dream,
Unheeding now alike men's praise and blame.
To all the world her name is but a name
It will forget, to-morrow, or more soon.
To-day she is so pale, her face doth seem
A little flower underneath the moon.

Her eyelids fallen o'er her sweet, still eyes,
Like leaves shut round two violets that are dead.
Those eyes will gaze no more astonishèd,
Nor grief will touch, nor tears will make less
    bright.
So young she died, like snow that hardly lies
One hour on earth for being too pure and white.

If she could speak again, what would she say
Of what white days in what forgotten Springs?
What sudden birds with Summer on their wings?
What thoughts too pure for any earth of ours?

She fell asleep so early on the way,
With eyes still full of dreams and hands of flowers.

She died too young to know the weary years
Of unfulfilled and incompleted bliss.
O dear, dead child, you will not grieve for this,
Nor see the darkness fall where sunshine gleams,
Nor lose your stars through eyes grown dim with
 tears . . .
She was too young to know her dreams were
 dreams.

O peaceful eyes, we are more wise than you,
In that we know all dreams must pass away;
For evil is upon us while we pray,
And sorrow is upon us when we smile—
Alas! beneath a sky so pure and blue
What evil and what sorrow all the while.

We learn life's truths—through sorrow growing wise;
We see men sow for other men to reap;
We see men laugh, while by their side men weep,
And good and evil side by side draw breath . . .
But you are far more wise, O peaceful eyes,
In that you know the mystery of Death.

MOONLIGHT

THE moonlight shimmers on the water's breast.
The stars above look down like glorious eyes
That view the quiet world with sad surprise;
The great, wide world that lieth still at rest.
The dew falls fast upon the closing flower;
A distant bell chimes out the passing hour—
    The fleeting hour.

The moonlight quivers in the grassy lane;
Each flower awake within her soft green bed
Uplifts her heavy, dew-wet, fragrant head,
To catch the light that pours in silver rain.
The wind is whisp'ring in the tree-tops high,
Whose long arms seem to sweep the very sky—
    The starlit sky.

The moonlight falls with radiance, slender, fair,
Within a church-yard silent as the dead ·
That sleep forever in their grassy bed,

6

And touches with soft fingers everywhere.
The wind is sighing on the grave's green breast,
And seems to murmur : "Here alone is rest—
      Is perfect rest."

A WINTER PIECE

A LITTLE while ago
The radiant Summer, with her azure eyes
And flower-crowned head, had shaken down a snow
Of lovely blossoms, fairer than the Spring,
Till these bare boughs were white and glittering,
And wild, sweet, panting birds stopped here to sing
A little while ago.

As if a passing cloud
Let loose some flakelets from his downy breast,
To hide thy bareness in a dazzling shroud,
O tree, the blossoms fell! More fair than these
Are not foam-flakes that whiten Summer seas,
Frail blossoms drifted by a lang'rous breeze
As from a passing cloud.

Where are these blossoms now?
Answer, wild winds and ghostly Winter, king
Who reigneth with white beard and ice-bound brow.

Alas, alas! poor tree, so gaunt and bare,
Sad skies, cold snows, and silence ev'rywhere;
Only thy mournful whisper stirs the air,
      "Where are my blossoms now?" . . .

     A little while ago
I knew a young child-heart, as free from care,
And pure and perfect as pale fallen snow,
Full of sweet dreams — "Spring buds are never
    dead,
And Summer follows fast on Summer's tread;
The world is good, and men are true," she said
     A little while ago.

     This heart is wiser now.
Her dreams are shattered, lightly blown away,
Like Summer blossoms from a Summer bough.
Like thee, O tree, whose buds with Spring are gone,
The heart that lost its dreams with youth's gold
    dawn
In life's pathetic winter-time must mourn:
     "Where are my blossoms now?"

WHO KNOWS?

WHAT does the south wind tender say to thee,
  Rosebud red, rosebud fair?
What does the sunbeam golden say to thee,
  Darting here, darting there?
What does the pearly dewdrop say to thee?
      The perfumed air,
      The moon's pale ray—
      What do they say?

I hold thee close that I may hear thine answer,
  Rosebud small, rosebud sweet;
That I may catch each word till all thine answer
  Be complete, quite complete;
That I may catch each low and tender whisper
      Passing fleet.
      Tell me, I pray,
      What do they say?

No fragrant whisper stirs thy crimson petals,
  No sigh, no faintest sigh;

Perhaps they fold the secret safe among them,
  Those leaves, as warm they lie
Around thy heart, and till they open widely
        By-and-by—
        Safe hid away,
        There it shall lay.

And when at last in full-blown, dewy splendor,
  Bud no more, flower rare,
Shalt thou then waft thy closely hidden secret
  On the warm Summer air,
Until some cloudlet near the sunset golden,
        Still and fair,
        The secret hears,
        And melts to tears?

Perhaps thou wilt impart it, rosebud tender,
  To some bird singing near—
Flinging out his joyous song, full-throated,
  Loud and sweet, loud and clear.
And will it be the burden of his song then,
        Flower dear?
        O silent rose,
        Who knows, who knows?

LITTLE HAND

CLASP mine closer, little, dear, white Hand—
  Clasp mine fastly, till it grows so cold
All your tender pressures will be vain
To awake an answ'ring touch again,
  Till it lieth underneath the mould.

I remember how I saw you first,
  Little Hand. Against the cottage wall
Grew a spray of honeysuckle, till
It had reached and touched your lattice sill,
  And there, saucily, it seemed to call

For your touch to recompense its toil.
  Oh, I thought the spray was very bold!
'Twixt the silken curtains soft you crept,
Little Hand, and all my heart upleapt
  As you plucked that long, pale spray of gold.

I remember how I kissed you first—
  It was underneath the stars of June,

On that day whose mem'ry lingers sweet.
You were lying on the old stone seat,
  Wrought to marble pureness by the moon.

Cold as marble till I clasped you close,
  And those little fingers softly kist—
All the passion throbbing in my soul,
Overflowed into that kiss that stole
  Up where lies that ring of amethyst.

Did you tremble when you felt that touch?
  Did it thrill you, little fingers fair?
I have laid it sacredly—that day—
In the wards of memory—the way
  Mothers lay a dead child's locks of hair.

Little Hand, creep closer, let me feel
  With my hand that grows, alas, so cold—
Let me softly feel that finger where
With love's first, most holy kiss you wear
  Graciously that sacred band of gold.

In Life's storm, and in Life's sun, 'tis you
  Who have guided me throughout the land—

Straightly—where the path was most obscure,
Purely, for who touches you is pure—
  Little Hand, O little lovèd Hand.

It is you who held the cup of bliss
  To my lips till I had drank my fill;
It is you who opened to me wide
Love's gold portals where all joys abide,
  Where we linger, and shall linger still.

What! all wet with tears? Nay, little Hand,
  Our farewell is only for a while;
I will watch you from the other shore,
I will wait you, patient, till once more
  I can clasp you 'neath God's holy smile.

Paradise without you could not be.
  I will wait outside till I behold
You appear; and if God will, dear Hand,
'Twill be you who clasps mine where I stand,
  'Twill be you who opes the Gates of Gold.

7

A PORTRAIT

WHEN she singeth through the silence,
Springeth music as of birds—
And the birds have no songs sweeter
Than the music of her words.
If she sings where no birds be,
Still the silent place rejoices,
Bird-forsaken, for her voice is
What a rose's voice might be.

When she smileth you go thinking
Of the Spring in Winter days.
Crocus-cups and pale primroses—
Sunshine through a leafy maze ;
Snow-drops where the snow-drifts be—
Spring in all midwinter places
You go finding—for her face is
What a new Spring's face might be.

When you know her you must love her,
Certes, love her like a star ;

She is lifted far above you—
Very fair and very far.
She will smile for you and me,
But not love. Her soul apart is
With the flowers; and her heart is
What a white star's heart might be.

ODE TO A NIGHTINGALE

Husш ! I hear the nightingale's pure notes,
Faint and far,
Like a star
That from out the depth of heaven floats.
So from out the foliage, dense and green,
Floats the music of the nightingale ;
In a rapture of delight
For the gloaming dim and white,
In a rhapsody of love for chaste Dian, pure and
pale.

Ev'ry flower 'neath the moon's mild dart
Lifteth up
Pearl-dewed cup
To receive the song into her heart ;
And the breeze hath caught it in his arms,
Flinging it and floating it afar.
O thou wondrous nightingale !
Am'rous of the moonlight pale,
Hast thou learnt thy song divine from the music
of the star ?

What sweet theme, Bird, moveth thee to sing?
　　　　Star or flower?
　　　　Moonlit hour?
Joy or grief? or beauty of the Spring?
Did thy song have birth in floods of love?
Art thou love-embodied? All the earth
　　　　Ringeth with thy clear refrain,
　　　　Floating like a mystic rain,
Upward to the star's unrest, downward to the
　　flower's birth.

Hearing, I forget that Life is pain,
　　　　That the morrow
　　　　Brings forth sorrow,
And that dear, dead buds bloom not again.
Oh, to lie, as now, forevermore,
With this music swelling out so sweet!
　　　　But all things must cease to be,
　　　　And thy tender rhapsody
Melteth with the drooping star, as all joys are,
　　incomplete.

Certes, Bird, thy song has source elsewhere.
　　　　Here, alas,
　　　　Pleasures pass

Fleet of foot, and joys, heart - grievings bear.
Friends grow cold, and even Love forgets;
Flowers fade, and Spring dies very soon;
  Beauty passeth in a breath,
  And Life yields itself to Death,
And the wonder of thy voice fadeth with the
 fading moon.

Memory of joy's sweet ecstasy,
  Love's first kiss,
  Love's best bliss,
Were not worthy of thy melody.
Doth thy song express some hidden dream,
Deep, too deep for words, within man's heart?
  Some vague longing, some unrest,
  Some sweet vision unexpressed
Of a world where Summer lives and dear friends
 must never part.

Bird, thy song into my spirit creeps!
  What were Night,
  Stars and Light,
Lacking music that from thee outleaps?
Dulcet notes that overflow the world,
Piercing clouds and darkness like a knife,

In a mellow‑flooding breath
That is worth all Life and Death . . .
And so Love's sweet song o'erflows all the solemn
dirge of Life.

MYSTERY

WHAT do you hide, O treacherous smooth ocean,
　　Beneath your breast where vagrant breezes roam,
Kissing the hollowed waves to sweet emotion
　　That breaks into a thousand flakes of foam?

Have you some treasure 'neath your bosom sleep-
　　　　ing,
　　Upon the shores ere long to lie decreed?
Is there some perfect pearl within your keeping,
　　Or is there only some sad, strange sea-weed?

O sea of Life! O Future, that is bidden
　　To hold your secret like the heaven's floor,
Have you some treasure in your bosom hidden,
　　To fling erelong upon my sun-stained shore?

I watch and wonder as long billows, creeping,
　　Divide and nearer roll with noiseless speed.
Is there some perfect pearl within your keeping,
　　Or is there only some sad, strange sea-weed?

MORS ET VITA

A church-yard—aye, but Spring had shaken down
    Her roses like a shower of sweet snow;
      There was a bird where'er a bird could sing,
    There was a rose where'er a rose could grow,
      And all the long, pale grass smelt sweet of
        Spring.

The trees had leaves half shut, like dreams half
      dreamed,
    And here a bird and there a bud was set;
      A linnet sang so sweetly overhead,
    So glad and sweet, 'twas easy to forget
      That underneath the roses lay the dead.

Two maidens stood there in the radiant noon:
    One plucked the roses, fair as they were frail,
      And mingled with the birds her happy breath;
    The other pondered, thoughtful-browed and pale,
      Upon that mystery which men call Death.
8

DECEPTION

O Bird,
Sweet, sorrowful swallow speeding to the south,
Ah, was it so?
Didst leave thy home because a rose's mouth
Told thee to go—
Because a rose's mouth,
Blown red in the warm South,
Told thee sweet Spring, white-browed, with violet
eyes,
Into the North had fled, and thou must go?
Didst follow her because thy heart was stirred
By one red rose's word,
O Bird?

Poor Bird—
Thou found'st the rose had spoken false to thee.
Spring still is far,
The frost-bound earth puts forth no bloom for thee,
The sky no star.

A wild wind hurts thy breast,
A snow-drop fills thy nest.
O sorrowful, sweet swallow, speed away,
Back to thy South a while.   Aye, that is best.
Back o'er the flower - flecked meadows, zephyr-
   stirred,
      Back to thy South, O Bird,
        Poor Bird !

        Poor Heart !
Since thou and I have left our soft sweet South
        Joy turned to woe.
False were the words from that false smiling mouth
        That bid us go ;
       That promised we should find
       White stars and whisp'ring wind,
And shining daffodils and golden moons.
But we have found bleak skies and harsh winds
   drear.
O sorrowful, sweet swallow-bird, depart;
Thine is the gladdest, ours the saddest part.
We cannot follow thee, I and my Heart,
        Poor Heart !
   And Spring comes never here.

MISCONCEPTION

A SONG.

There's a bee in the rose,
Though you cannot see it,
Stealing her sweet, stealing her sweet.
Nobody knows
There's a bee in the rose
Under their feet, under their feet.
Wafts of south breezes have stirred her to motion.
See! she is bathed in the sun's golden ocean.
Who could divine it?
Nobody knows
There's a bee in the rose.

There's a grief in my heart,
Though you cannot see it,
Darkening love's light—darkening love's light.
How you would start
If you looked in my heart,
All is such dreary and desolate night.

Still I go smiling, eyes bright with emotion,
Gazing, you think, on Joy's mystical ocean.
      Sweet misconception !
   How you would start
   If you looked in my heart !

SUNRISE

A SONNET

A sudden trembling through the star's repose,
A thrill of light pulsing at Night's dark breast,
Till Dawn's dim promise is made manifest—
Pale, like the leaves around a folded rose.
All the wan stars swarm back and melt as those
Low, pallid lights rise seething, unsuppressed,
Stirred like the white foam on a green wave's crest,
Till all the sky is like a budding rose.
But the red bar of light that throbs and glows
Breaks of a sudden, and the cloud-flakes start,
Curling with their faint, pink-flushed rims apart,
Like the dropped petals of a full-blown rose,
Till the sun springs up where the skies unclose
Like the gold centre of the rose's heart.

WHITE ROSES

THERE was a rose-tree grew so high
And white with all its seven roses,
It seemed a cloud 'twixt earth and sky.

There was one rose among the seven
That grew alone on topmost bough,
Like a white star caught down from heaven.

I plucked it that it should not be
Deflowered by rainy, wild west winds
In all its white virginity. . . .

There was a little maiden dead
In a dark room in a lone place—
Two candles at her feet and head.

Her two hands crossed upon her breast,
Like frail rose petals, but more still—
Glad to be folded thus at rest.

Her pale lips smiling all the while,
In such a solemn, perfect peace,
Alas, as our lips never smile.

I gave my white rose to the dead—
It seemed less white than her young brow. . . .
The others wept—"Alas!" they said.

I gave my white rose to the child,
Both plucked in their young purity. . . .
And while the others wept I smiled.

HEART SONGS

ON the wall there clambered a wild white rose,
A wild white rose with a dainty face ;
She climbed and climbed, till with even's close
She reached a window. Perhaps—who knows?—
She had chosen that as her resting‑place,
For there at the casement she crept, until
Her head drooped over the window-sill.

And in the window, through all the Spring,
There hung a bird in a sad repose.
Said the wond'ring rose : "Dost thou never sing ?"
Said the mournful bird: "But of what sweet thing
Shall I make my song? Oh, thou foolish rose !
Shall I sing the loneness that all days hold,
Or my captive state in this cage of gold ?

"The skylark sings to the rosy dawn ;
The nightingale sings to the silver stars.
I never look on the early morn,
And when at even the stars are born,

9

I see them only across these bars;
And so," said the bird in the window-sill,
"I am always mournful and always still."

And the wild white rose, as the bird's grief hushed,
Widened her petals so far apart
Against the prison of gold they brushed,
And the dainty face of the white rose blushed
Till the pale pink faded into her heart.
The white rose blushed as she murmured: "See!
Am I not so fair you can sing for me?"

Then a great joy came to the little bird—
A joy that spilled from his quiv'ring throat
In sweetest music was ever heard;
The hearts that listened were strangely stirred
By the love and passion in every note.
"Whence cometh this music?" they said. "Who
      knows?"
But no one noticed the wild white rose.

When Autumn swept, with her brown-breast thrush,
And her robes aflame, o'er the distant hill,
To set on fire each tree and bush,
In the little cage reigned a mournful hush,

And the small brown bird was sad and still.
"Whence cometh this silence? Who knows?"
    they said;
But no one noticed the rose was dead.

Who knows? "This singer sings sweet," you say,
"Across his prison of grief and pain.
Why does he sing so? His skies are gray,"
Or, "This one," you whisper, "is still to-day,
And his music will never flow again."
Who knows the reason?
        But who has said
What rose is living—what rose is dead?

SONNET

A POET wrote a song—a tender lay—
Of Life that dies, and Love that ne'er is dead.
"Life is the setting, Love the jewel," he. said ;
And then he tossed it carelessly away.
A south wind passing, heard it softly say:
"O save me! save me from this cold, hard bed !"
And caught it up, and soaring with it, fled
Up, up into the cloudlets dim and gray,
Then down again, and laid it on a tree.
A little, plain, brown bird came flying by,
Sighing : "Ah, Fate has been most harsh to me,
I cannot charm the ear or please the eye !"
She found the song, and in the moonlight pale
She sang it through—it was the nightingale !

A THOUGHT

THERE are some pearls which lie beneath the sea—
      So deep, so deep,
No diver's hand can reach, nor eye behold.
      The waters keep
Their treasure safely hid and all untold.
Through years and years, through storms that o'er
    it whirl,
  Fairer than other pearls, perhaps, this pearl.

There are some thoughts which lie within the soul—
      So far, so far ;
So deep within the heart's most secret cell,
      Like some hid star,
That but this heart its whispers sweet can tell.
Safe hid away and treasured and unsought,
Fairer than other thoughts, perhaps, this thought.

WINTER-TIME

My little love, the winter-time is nigh;
The months of rose and moon and nightingale
    Have faded with the leaves;
The wasted trees stand ghost-like 'gainst the sky—
The little nests are empty in the eaves,
       The flowers are pale,
And all the skies are desolate above,
       O little love!

The flowers are pale, with fallen leaves between,
And rainy, wild east winds go floating by,
    Whirling the dead, dry grass.
O yellow forest leaf! once young and green,
How swift thy Spring did pass, as all things pass
    From earth and sky.
There is a sadness in the field and dale,
    And flowers are pale.

From earth and sky the sweetness of the Spring
Hath passed—as flowers below, as stars above—

And from my heart the same.
But I lose more than birds that cease to sing,
Than roses, fading swifter than they came.
O little love!
And all this sweet returneth by-and-by
To earth and sky.

O little love, my winter-time hath come,
The years of youth, of faith, of dreams are fled;
They faded with the leaves.
So many dear, loved voices have grown dumb,
So many nests are empty in the eaves—
So much is dead!
Ah! earth has many springs, but we have one. . . .
. . . And mine is done.

.

ABSENCE

A SHADOWY sail upon a smooth, sweet sea. . . .
Alas, that sail is lost for evermore!
And it hath borne thee very far from me,
    Upon this shore.

Since then all days are weary Winter days,
Though blithe birds sing through shadowy Sum-
    mer moons;
Since then all Springs bring unenchanted Mays
    And roseless Junes.

MAY

Come, dear, for it is May. Leave work and book,
And I will lead you to so sweet a nook
Whose green leaves make a little tender night,
    With flowers for stars.
A thrush sings there, but singeth out of sight,
And a brook's silver feet run very near.
    Come, dear.

The breeze will stir a bed of leaves for you,
And show some shy wood-violet, freshly blue;
Or through leaf-tangled boughs a patient bird
    On a brown nest.
And from the grass which the bold breeze has stirred
We will pluck violets first of all the year.
    Come, dear.

Come, dear; leave book and work these fair May
    hours;
The grass is pale with delicate, frail flowers. . . .
10

What can a book say which can be so sweet
As a bird's song?
Or as white blossom-faces 'neath our feet?
When blossom-faces tire mine will be near.
Come, dear.

"I HAVE NO SPRING," SHE SAITH

PANTOUM

THE white buds drift along the leas,
    The daffodils are tall and bold,
Pale foam-flowers tremble on the seas,
    The sun fills hollowed waves with gold.

The daffodils are tall and bold,
    The brook flows like a crystal tear;
All things are fair, which were so cold,
    All things are glad which were so drear.

The brook flows like a crystal tear,
    On either side rose-petals fall;
A pale, frail maiden standeth here,
    Alas! who hath no Spring at all.

On either side rose-petals fall,
    With sound of song the hushed grass hears,
The pale, frail maid doth gaze on all
    With eyes that are too sad for tears.

With sound of song the hushed grass hears,
   Rose - petal falleth silently ;
As one whose heart beats low with fears,
   The maid doth sigh—sad sigheth she.

"O rose - leaf, falling silently,
   O linnet, with glad, singing breath,
My love is far—is far from me,
   And so I have no Spring," she saith.

TO EDITH

EDITH, it seems to me life is so brief
  That half of joy doth lie in memory,
  Like 'a bird singing that we cannot see,
Like a pale flower folded in a leaf,
    Is memory.

Something we have, yet cannot touch nor hold,
  That once has been, yet never more will be ;
  Like moonlight shadows on a Summer sea,
Like many clouds which many stars unfold,
    Is memory.

Life is so short ! It is a little sleep,
  And all joys leave us, swift as swallows flee . .
  When these days pass, so dear to you and me,
Yet half their joy, my friend, we still may keep
    Through memory.

" ROSE ET NOIR "

"ROSE ET NOIR"

"OH, generous, sweet Life!" I said,
Because—as on a silver thread
    We string white pearls—Life, bliss on bliss
Had strung together. Thus complete
I held them, till my heart's quick beat
Grew quicker. Do you wonder, Sweet,
    That I was glad for this?

I do not know from whence the touch
That shook my white pearls overmuch,
    And snapped the string. Then bliss on bliss
Slipped through my fingers on the sand—
Alone was left within my hand
A broken thread. You understand
    I have been sad since this.

11

Oh, moonlight spider-web,
　　Filmy and fine and fair!
A cloud of dew-drops blown
From rose-hearts overgrown—
　　Transfixed upon the bosom of the air.

Oh, moonlight-colored web,
　　That some rude hand has torn!
Each broken, lifeless thread
Hangs downward, gray and dead,
　　Caught on the sharp edge of a red-rose
　　　　thorn.

Oh, frail, fine web of Life,
　　Woven 'mid stars above,
Shattered on earth one day!
Mine lieth dead and gray,
　　Caught on the sharp edge of the Thorn of
　　　　Love.

SPRING's hands are always full of rosy flowers,
　Unopened buds to deck each field and tree.
We love and watch them through the long, sweet
　　hours,
　Not for the buds, but what the buds will be.

Life's hands are full of buds. She comes on sing-
　　ing,
　With radiant eyes, across Youth's golden gate;
We smile to see the burden she is bringing,
　And for the Summer are content to wait.

When Summer comes with sweet fulfilling hours,
　Our hearts expand beneath Hope's brightest
　　beams . . .
Do all the buds bloom into perfect flowers?
　Does the fulfilment realize our dreams?

Alas! those dreams long cherished with affection—
　Alas! those smiling eyes where tears are born—
So many buds die ere they reach perfection;
　So many, opened, show the hidden thorn.

In a field of daffodils,
Which their golden sunlight fills,
    I love roaming
    In the gloaming,
Through the yellow daffodils.

All the fire-flies come out,
Whirl and dance and flit about.
    Golden showers
    Fill the hours
When the fire-flies come out.

Daffodils are not so fair
Nor so yellow as her hair.
    Brighter eyes—
    Fire-flies—
Greet me—meet me—soon somewhere!

She is waiting by the gate,
Come I early, come I late;
    Two hands meeting—
    Two hearts beating . . .
Ask it of the old wood gate.

I WONDER, in those dear old days departed,
  Whose was the foot that wore this tiny shoe—
A slipper just as small as Cinderella's,
  But not of glass—of faded satin blue.

I'll say it was a princess, tall and stately,
  And rather haughty, but not overmuch.
I see her walking through her garden alleys:
  How rose-hearts beat to feel that light foot's
    touch!

I see her treading through her row of pages,
  That small foot lifted high with haughty grace;
A knight beside her, whisp'ring tender speeches—
  She hears them all, with silent, downcast face.

I see her in the dazzling ball-room, stepping
  Through stately minuet or swifter dance,
Her small foot slipping through her rich robes
    sweeping,
  Or even not perceived—divined, perchance.

How many knights adored you, little Slipper,
  And knelt before you—fine and fair and blue!
How many you have fled from—too bold suitors!
How many hearts you've trod on, tiny Shoe!

Do as the bee does, my Heart,
  Hov'ring where pale bud blows ;
Flitting where petals part,
Stealing, where sunbeams dart,
  Only the sweets of the rose.
Do as the bee does, my Heart.

The fairest rose has her thorn !—
  Come when the dew is wet—
Steal all her sweets at morn,
Leave her ere nightshades dawn.
  Do as the bee does : forget
The fairest rose has her thorn.

You dear, quaint garden with your old-time
    flowers,
  Deep purple pansies and sweet mignonette,
' A bed of primrose, meek and pensive blowing,
Small silver daisies and shy violets growing
  With upraised faces, fresh and wild and wet.

Were I the sun, I'd always shine upon you,
  And kiss those pansy faces, quaint and bright.
Were I the dew, I'd cling in pearly showers,
And never leave you—frail, delicious flowers ;
  Were I the moon, I'd light you all the night.

Were I the wind, I'd steal your violets' perfume;
  Were I the sky, I'd always smile above you ;
Were I a bird, I'd only sing your praises ;
Were I a bee, I'd only woo your daisies . . .
  But I'm a mortal, and can only love you!

Do you remember how that night was sweet?
  You called it sweet and something more as
    well.
The fine white moonbeams drifted at our feet,
  And nestled in each flower's trembling bell.

The hollowed waves came creeping to the beach,
  And broke there with a joyful sound at last.
Do you remember how there was no speech?
  No need for that. Our heart-beats throbbed
    too fast.

A small white falling star shot through the gray.
  You bid me "wish!" before it could depart.
Do you remember how I answered, "Nay?"
  Because there was no wish left in my heart.

12

JUST a multitude of curls
Weighing down a little head;
Two wide eyes not blue nor gray,
Like the sky 'twixt night and day,
Small red mouth—and all to say
      IIas been said.

Just a saucy word or glance,
And a hand held out to kiss;
Just a curl—a ribbon through—
Just a flower—fresh and blue. . . .
And to think what men will do—
      Just for this!

OVER the West there the moon is afloat
On a pale-green sea in a silver boat.
She has set on fire her Night-bird's throat,
That grows more perfect with every note.

The scent-burdened zephyrs awake again—
The night dew is falling in purple rain—
There's a star so fair that each rose must fain
Confess her passion. In vain! in vain!

A great white moth like a little moon,
Is waking a flower asleep too soon,
And bidding her hark to the Night-bird's tune...
Oh, ev'rything's sweet in the month of June!

THISTLEDOWN

I BEAR three flowers shrined in my heart of
    hearts. . . .

When on the first I look, which is a rose,
I see a Star, and hear two birds that sing;
When on the next, a pale anemone,
I see a white hand with a golden ring;
When on the last, which is a dead wild weed,
I see a green grave in the heart of Spring.

———

To lean o'er the water's edge where the tall reeds
    lean
        With the stars between
        In the water's sheen
           Twice seen.

To stand knee-deep in the clover with mild-eyed cows
        Who dream and browse
        Where the small birds drowse
          On the boughs.

To lie and to dream and forget in the golden wheat,
Where the poppies meet
And the breezes greet. . . .
This is sweet,
Sweet !

———

THERE'S a bird beneath your window;
There's a sunbeam that slips in;
There's a rose-bush in your garden
Where a spider learns to spin.

And we're all in league against you—
Bird and rose and gold sun-dart—
And the web the spider's spinning
Is the mesh to hold your heart.

I WAS your friend once, very long ago.
You held the key wherewith to ope my heart,
What did you find there? Aught of sin or woe?...
A host of flowers 'neath a mild sun's dart.

I am your friend again. Now take this key—
Unlock my heart once more and step therein.
What do you find? The flowers that used to be?...
A tangled bed of weeds of grief and sin!

———

Do you remember, long ago,
When as a child you bound me fast
With daisy-chains, and would not let me go?

O daisies, you are dead, 'tis true,
But still I'm bound as fast to-day,
With chains I cannot break so soon as you.

———

I PUT my Heart in a bell.
"Now ring, now ring," I said,
"So every one may hear
    My love is dead."

I gave my Heart to a bird.
"Now sing it out," I said,
"So all who list may know
    My love is dead."

I gave my Heart to a flower.
"Who plucks shall find," I said,
"The flower hides a heart
Whose love is dead."

THERE's a flush on the face of the apple-trees;
There are buds and blossoms and leaves all over.
The bees have found—oh, the small wise bees!—
There's a green lane full of the sweet red clover.

My love is a maid with a rose for her mouth,
And I hear her voice when the linnets sing.
My love is a dream from the soft, sweet South;
My love is a maid, and her name is Spring.

In her hand
She takes a rose—
A rare rose from the South,
Like a little red shut mouth,
And the folded leaves unclose.
O rose,
Poor rose !

In her hand
She takes my heart—
The heart that I thought to keep,
And the love I had hid so deep
Unfolds, as the rose-leaves part.
O heart,
Poor heart!

———

WINTER

THE bare trees look like spectres in a shroud;
  The day-old snow, half melted into rain,
  Lies in wet pools along the misty plain;
The wan moon peeps out from a fleeting cloud.

The bleak winds fleet by with their mournful
    wail;
  And low and slow a lone bird loiters by,
  Breaking the silence with his shrill, sad cry . . .
Ah, Winter's face looks lean and pinched and
    pale.

SPRING

THE bud that looked out with a wistful smile
    Has shrunk back in the gray, cold earth to die.
    O swallows, swallows, fleeting in the sky,
Go back to your warm, sunny South a while. . . .

. . . Lo! from the cloud-hearts golden daggers leap!
    Spring woke just now and smiled with her red
        mouth:
    Nay, swallows, swallows, speeding to the South,
Turn back—Spring is not dead; she was asleep.

SUMMER

THE low, large moon lies in the liquid sky,
    And breathless stars are watching her from
        far . . .
    So I should watch, if I were but a star,
The lanquid-eyed, sweet Summer fleeting by.

A white, frail-petaled rose is at her breast—
  Ere the closed leaves have folded back and
    shown
  The great gold gleaming heart, the rose has
    flown . . .
Summer is dead . . . the moon dropped from the
  West.

———

AUTUMN

She kindles fires in every tree and bush—
  The thicket flames with gold and crimson-
    red—
  To keep bleak Winter far ere she is dead.
Thus Autumn fades off in a splendid flush.

A fainter, paler sun burns in her skies;
  Her leaves at last drop off by one, by one—
  Like the dull ashes of the fire that's done—
Then Autumn draws her gray hood close and
  dies.

O Pepita! my Pepita!
  Who would wish you fairer, brighter?
Would you make the roses sweeter?
  Would you paint the lily whiter?

Nay, Pepita, my Pepita!
  Your blue eyes could not be bluer;
Your sweet face could not be sweeter;
  But your small heart might be truer.

———

The moon sits far in the heaven,
  And spins where the shadows ebb.
The golden stars, one here, one there,
  Are souls caught in her web.

———

If I could steal your wings
  When you were through with them,
Nightingale, nightingale,
  What would I do with them?

Fly to the golden South?
  Fly to the heaven?
Fly where the flowers blow
  Seven times seven?

If I could steal your wings
  When you were through with them,
Into her heart I'd fly—
  That's what I do with them.

———

I DREAMT I loved a Star,
  A Star so far above me;
She said: "It is in vain
  Men seek to know and love me."

I dreamt that I was dead.
  Methought that I was lying
Deep in a grave, deep down—
  The winds above me sighing.

In the darkness of the grave
I saw my Star below me.
She said: "My name is Peace,
And only here men know me."

————

THERE was a star
Which out of the height of heaven fell,
And was lost, ah me!
The beautiful star fell into the sea,
And falling, was folded into a shell,
And the beautiful star became a pearl
In the sea.

There was a smile
Which out of her eyes' blue heaven fell
As the sunbeams dart.
The beautiful smile fell into my heart,
And falling, was folded in Love's sweet shell,
And the beautiful smile became a song
In my heart.

The flowers take her for an April day,
　　She is so fair, and all her hair is gold.
The shy blue violets, when they see her, say,
　　"Her eyes are, like our sisters, grown bold."
The roses know she is more fair than they.

I watch her fleeting through the cool green grass
　　One moment, as a Summer breeze might fleet.
My heart and all the flowers watch her pass,
　　And when we cannot hear her little feet,
My heart and all the flowers sigh, "Alas!"
14

TRIOLETS

I

THE Summer is over,
　And song-birds are flying.
Oh, love me, thy lover,
For Summer is over ;
Pale buds and dead clover,
　And Love goes a-sighing,
When Summer is over,
　When song-birds are flying.

II

Her love was the dew
　And my heart was the flower.
Ah, wisely I knew
That her love was the dew,
For her kisses were few,
　And she loved me one hour.
Her love was the dew
　And my heart was the flower.

III

I never will forget that day,
  But you and Love forget it, sweet :
The green grass path, the rose-flowered way ;
I never will forget that day,
And all the things we had to say,
  And the old way we used to meet.
I never will forget that day,
  But you and Love forget it, sweet.

IV

There's a bird in the nest on the tree,
  Though the Spring-blooms pale and wither ;
There's a pearl in the deep of the sea,
Like the bird in the nest on the tree;
There's a Heart that is all for thee,
  Though no love-songs rise thither;
There's a bird in the nest on the tree,
  Though the Spring-blooms pale and wither.

V

Your Love and a Flower . . .
　And the Flower lived longest.
You gave me one hour
Your Love and a Flower,
And laughed at Time's power
　To slay love when strongest.
Your Love and a Flower,
　And the Flower lived longest.

VI

A snow - drop told me Spring was near,
　And so I'll make a song about her,
Of birds and buds and blue skies clear.
A snow - drop told me Spring was near—
But no, I'll wait until she's here,
　For till she's here, alas, I doubt her.
A snow - drop told me Spring was near,
　But I have made no song about her.

VII

A primrose in a green leaf set,
  Though no bird sings in any tree.
Chill Winter is not dead, but yet
The primrose in a green leaf set
(Of which I make this triolet)
  Brings thoughts of Spring to you and me.
A primrose in a green leaf set,
  Though no bird sings in any tree.

VIII

The sweet, blue iris stars the stream,
  And green woods are alive with song.
The wild, pink-petaled roses dream,
The sweet, blue iris stars the stream,
And two gold-throated linnets seem
  To sing their hearts out all day long.
The sweet, blue iris stars 'the stream,
  And green woods are alive with song.

IN TUSCANY

MINOR NOTES

(TWELVE RISPETTI)

I

I SEARCH among the flowers in the grass,
  And in the trees, and in the new, young Spring,
For I have lost a little Heart, alas!
  A little Heart which was so sweet a thing.
And all day long I move my weary feet,
Seeking the little Heart which was so sweet;
And all night long I wander with the wind,
Seeking the little Heart I cannot find.

II

I am a faded leaf, and you a flower,
  A fresh young flower, set in a nest of green.
The Spring is here, and she has made a bower
  Of buds and leaves, with birds that sing between.
I am a faded leaf, a foolish thing
To live on still in all this joyous Spring;
And when I fall, whose days have been so brief,
Who will be sad, or miss a faded leaf?

15

III

If I could choose a gift for thee, dear Heart,
  I should not choose the fairest things there are
In gems or gold, but I should choose, dear Heart,
  A Tuscan day to send to thee afar.
A Tuscan day which is a thing so sweet
That it would teach thy English heart to beat;
A Tuscan day which is so sweet a thing
When it is plucked from out the heart of Spring.

IV

My Flower you would haply call a weed,
  Beneath a tree so sad and dark it grows;
A little Flower which would fade indeed,
  Beside a spring-time lily or a rose.
I love my Flower, which all others shun,
Because its life hath known no light or sun.
My Flower, hidden where the dark leaves part,
I love because it is so like my heart.

V

I ride through forest and I ride through dale,
  Made dim and dark by many a tall pine-tree;

I sing my song, and hear the nightingale,
  Who is my little brother, answer me.
We sing a song that hath the same refrain,
And saith, alas! how Love is only pain;
That saith, alas! how like a thorn is Love
To men below and nightingales above.

VI

O Lisabella, dost thou bid me praise
  Thy rose-red lips and all thy wealth of hair?
Nay, should I sing them in a thousand ways,
  The world would never know how thou art
    fair.
The Spring will better praise thee, for she knows
Thy face is fairer than her fairest rose.
Her sweetest rose less fair is than thou art;
Her sharpest thorn is softer than thy heart.

VII

My Flower of Life bloomed into love and song
  That time I met him 'neath an olive-tree;
He was so fair, my love, so fair and strong!
  He broke an olive-branch and gave it me.

He gave it me, and bade it be a sign
Of all his love, which henceforth would be mine.
The olive-branch is here, but where is he? ...
My eyes are full of tears. I cannot see.

VIII

"My Heart," I said (it was a white Spring day,
　　With sweet wild birds adrift among the green)—
I said, "My Heart, our flowers are dead and gray,
　　Faint memories of the Summers that have been;
So let us from the fields new flowers bring." ...
I plucked a rose fresh from the heart of Spring;
I wonder why it is less sweet to me
Than last year's rose, which is a memory?

IX

I saw a grave beneath a cypress-tree,
　　Forgotten, with no cross, no name, no prayer.
But Spring remembered what men would not see,
　　And, like white angels' smiles, set flowers there.
The blithe birds passed across with songs of Spring,
And where men would not pause they paused to
　　sing.

Where no men prayed, the moonlight was a
 prayer . . .
I would that grave were mine, and I were there.

X

I sometimes have strange fancies in the Spring.
 I think the birds we hear—sweet, fleeting birds—
Have stole from poet-hearts the songs they sing
 Ere poet-lips have shaped them into words.
I think the frail white flowers on my way
Are sweet lost thoughts or dreams that are astray;
And all the poppies that are frail and red,
I think are tears some broken heart has shed.

XI

I leave the fields with all their bold bright flowers,
 With all their mellow sun and song of streams,
To seek the woods that have calm twilight hours—
 The sleeping woods, whose birds are spoken
  dreams.
I leave the fields to such as smile and sing,
To such as find new joys in the new Spring.
I leave the new Spring joys to the young leas,
And bring my old dead joys to the old trees.

XII

I heard a voice among the olive-trees,
　A singing voice beneath a Tuscan sky;
So sweet it drifted to me on the breeze,
　So sweet, I paused until the voice went by.
Like some white bird straight from the sunlit West
That brings its joy to a forsaken nest,
Into my heart, like some white bird, the breeze
Hath brought the song from out the olive-trees.

IN FLORENCE

O Tuscan days, my true, gold-hearted days,
With thy deep skies and fleecy clouds afloat,
Like the dropped petals of some moon-pale flower;

With thy still sunset, zephyr-stirrèd hour,
Thy evening bird with thrilled melodious throat...
Gone, gone from me, my golden Tuscan day.

Once wert thou with me in fair Florence, crown
Of all that perfect, flower-filled Italy.
Thy name, O Florence, like a song doth fill

With memories the gray unblossoming still
That girts me round and holds me fast from thee—
From thee, O peaceful, perfect Tuscan town.

Thy lang'rous hush at even-tide just stirred
By some faint convent chime from very far,
Thy murmurous Arno speeding on its way,

And in the East a shadow wan and gray,
Kindled to brightness by a single star,
And somewhere in the West a singing bird.

All mem'ries. And the window whence my eyes
Saw Ponte Vecchio with its old-time mien,
Like some rich gem set deep in thy gold heart;

And faint Fiesole, where pale clouds start,
Dusted with leafy olive-trees, gray-green,
That fade off in the shadow-girted skies.

O Florence, my fair Florence, I would stray
Once more to-day, as in that dear dead time,
Along the streets at golden mid-noon's hour,

Till thy old Duomo and thy slender tower
Rose up before me with its mid-noon chime,
And haply step therein. All twilight gray,

With a faint trail of incense on the air,
And the low murmured hidden monotone
Of priests at holy mass. So, entered in,

How still it seemed after the city's din,
How solemn sweet the organ's vibrant tone.
I did not pray. The silence was a prayer.

Then out again into the rain of gold
Flooding the broad gay piazza everywhere...
A flutter of white wings, a flock of birds

Let loose, like some sweet tumult of love words,
Floating and sweeping through the sun-cleft air,
To peck the golden grain some hands would hold.

In those Spring days (Spring comes with tend'rer
        look,
And far more lavish hands to that sweet place,
My little Tuscan town, than to this clime,

Cold England and its fogs) I used to climb
Thy Colli, Florence—climbing, reach the place
Where thy sweet face lies stretched out like a
        book ;

Lies stretched out like a soft smile, caught and kept
From the Past's fast-sealed lips, or like a flower
Yielding its petals up to the blue sky.
16

And when I strayed back to the city, I
Found all things flooded with the sunset hour
Save Ponte Vecchio, where the shadows crept.

Elsewise at night — the amorous Tuscan night,
When the white moon had climbed the silver
 stair
The fair stars make for their most lowly Queen—

How sweet from out the casement far to lean,
And feel the fragrance of the dewy air,
And see the whole world bathed in silver light!

Warm Tuscan sun! in that last dreaming lull
'Twixt night and day, along the Western ways
Thy tender light hath set from me fore'er:

Set, with my first lost love, lost dream, lost
 prayer . . .
O Tuscan days! my true, gold-hearted days,
Thy lips are dumb, and mine are sorrowful.

Thy earth beneath my feet is cold and brown,
The skies are netted in a blank, gray shroud,
The mournful rain is dripping from the eaves. . . .

Lost—like a flower too deep-sunk in the leaves;
Lost—like a white star hidden by a cloud,
I see thee now, O little Tuscan town!

A SEA-SPELL

THERE is a Siren in the sea,
And all day long she sings to me,
Until my soul is no more free.

I listen by the waves all day,
Although, if free, I should not stay
Beside a sea so cold and gray,

But choose a spot all sun and light,
With songs, and roses red and white,
And stars that make men love the night.

But all day long she sings to me
Of love that is a memory
More bitter than the bitter sea.

She sings to me of other years,
Nor will she cease until she hears
That she has drowned me in my tears.

IDYL

Along the sunny lane,
Wet with a fleeting rain,
And white with daisies in the tall green grass,
How sweet it is to stray
Throughout a Summer day,
Forgetting that a Summer day must pass.

White clover for the bee,
And just for you and me
A happy lark is singing in a bush,
Of Love and Stars and Spring,
And so we hear him sing,
Forgetting that the sweetest song must hush.

We have no thought or care,
Like all the flowers fair,
For any Morrow or for Yesterday;
And for a little while
How sweet it is to smile,
Forgetting that such smiles must pass away.

STORNELLI AND STRAMBOTTI

Stars in the sky!
My heart was like a heaven with all its stars
Until a wind arose, and swept them by.

*

O Wind, that hath my stars, come back to me,
    And place them in my heart as once before.
O dove-white Peace, give back, give back the key,
    That I may thus unlock thy fast-closed door.
O Love, why art thou like a bitter sea,
    Casting thy bitter weeds upon my shore?
O Stars, the wind hath drowned thee in that sea,
    And what is lost therein shall rise no more.

*   *   *

Roses in the shade!
You are so fair, and yet I pass you all,
Seeking a thornless rose that will not fade.

*   *   *

Foam o' the wave!
Here is my Heart; bear it to my lost love
Beneath the coral-reefs which are his grave.

*   *   *

O Hearts awake, the fields are all aglow
    With buttercups run through them like a flame,
The apple-trees have buds like flakes of snow,
    And flocks of wild, sweet birds no Spring can
        tame.
Theirs are the only songs I care to know—
    The sweetest songs that have no words or name.
O Hearts! go forth as birds do, even so,
    And sing your joy out boldly, without shame.

*   *   *

Lilacs in the grass!
Last time I plucked you he was at my side—
So little time it takes for love to pass.

*   *   *

At Lucca, in my garden, night comes bringing
    The sweetest nightingales that ever were.
I hear them first so very softly singing
    To make among the leaves a little stir;

But later, when the round white moon is flinging
  The cool gray shadows on each side of her,
I hear their songs through all the silence ringing,
  And dream, awake, of things that never were.

      *   *   *

O Love, thy face is pale as flowers are pale,
And thou hast hid an angel in thy heart,
And in thy throat thou hast a nightingale.

      *   *   *

I call my love *Rosina*, little rose;
  But yet in what rose-garden could you see
A flower fair as is the one that grows
  Rose-red upon the lips that smile for me?
Her brow is as the whiteness of the snows;
  Her eyes are as the color of the sea.
I call my love *Rosina*, little rose,
  Yet she is fairer far than roses be.

      *   -   *   *

Flower of Spring!
The moon is new, the bough has a new rose,
The heart new love, and birds new songs to sing.

      *

Oh, Rosinella, was it yesterday
That I was sad, aye, sad enough to weep?
To me it seems a year and more away.

*

Flower of bliss !
The poppies stain the grass like drops of blood,
And I have found a mouth as red to kiss.

17

*

ANITA

A BROAD green sea the vineyard lay;
IIe saw her pass along that way—
                    The fair Anita.

A little kerchief on her head;
A little mouth so small, so red,
                    IIad gay Anita.

Plaiting the straw and singing sweet,
He saw her with her bare brown feet—
                    The fair Anita.

"Oh, little joy of Spring," he said,
And kissed the mouth so small, so red,
                    Of gay Anita.

But when the ripened grapes had come
To stain the vines like purple foam
                    (Ah, poor Anita!)

He was not there; she did not sing;
And all the joy had fled from Spring
      For fair Anita.

Plaiting the straw with sweet lips dumb,
She waits, and yet he does not come—
      Alas, Anita!

SEA-BREEZE

THE keen sharp scent of the sea comes over the
    fields,
And brings me a thought of the silent, perilous
    sea;
Of the shadowy ship that is drifting away with
    thee;
That is bearing the face that I love so far from
    me,
Leaving me here alone with a memory
Of the joys that were and never more will be;
Of the hand that touched my hand so tenderly,
Of the voice that said "Farewell!" so mournfully.
These are the thoughts that come to me over the
    fields
With the breeze that brings me the keen sharp
    scent of the sea.

WHITE CLOVER

THE clover in the grass is white
  As little children's souls must be.
  The branches of the apple-tree
Sway in the mellow morning light.

More sweet than any spoken words
  I hear the singing meadow thrush,
  And after, in the breeze-stirred hush,
Dreams come to me like flocks of birds.

Among the clover in the lane,
  The thought comes of a Long Ago.
  And for a little while I know
I am a little child again.

SNOW-FLAKES

FOUR SONGS

I

THERE is one rose upon the bough—
One rose alone, for Spring hath passed—
I will not pluck that flower now,
    Because the last.

Ah me, I am less cruel than Death,
Who plucks the fairest flower that grows;
Who stripped my branches in a breath,
    And left no rose.

II

The silent sea and the long waste of sand
Look mystical and pale, and very dim,
Beneath the moon which hath a pallid gleam.

Beside this sea we wandered hand in hand.
He has forgot me. I remember him . . .
And all my Life is merged into a Dream.

III

A snow - flake out of the gray,
   And a leaf from a wild, white flower . . .
   A Love that lasted an hour,
A Joy that lasted a day.

One love hath faded away
   While the other love lives yet ;
   Oh, grief ! that one can forget,
And one remember for aye.

IV

A cloud of water - lilies
Beneath an evening star,
As pallid and as perfect
   As faces sometimes are.

As pallid and as perfect,
   And yet, alas, I know,
O lilies and O faces,
   The bitterness below.

TUSCAN HILLS

My Friend and I, we climbed together
Sweet - scented hill - sides covered over
With clusters of the lilac heather ;
Around us was the fair Spring weather.
She was my friend, I was her lover.

Above us was that perfect heaven
One only sees in Tuscany.
Below us was the valley, riven
With budding vineyards green and even,
Far - stretching like a Summer sea.

She heard sweet music from the thrushes,
I, from her voice, that softer grew
When swift the birds sprang from the bushes,
And in those sudden, tender hushes
We only talked as friends might do.

O scented hills we climbed together!
O blue, far sky that bent above her!
She never will forget that heather,
That Tuscan day, that soft Spring weather,
Yet me she has forgot—her lover.

18

DREAM-LAND

Once in a dream,
Between tall trees that had such golden flowers
As only blossom there ;
Beside a stream whose voice was as sweet showers,
And birds that sing between the twilight hours,
I saw a maid who was most wond'rous fair,
Once in a dream.

Upon her face
Was something of a never-fading Spring
And youth that will not die.
Her voice was as a thought of birds that sing
Close to the stars, and on her everything
Was white and pure, like clouds upon the sky
Or stainless snows.

And in my dream,
As lost Love's eyes, her eyes seemed even so . . .
"I am a wraith," she said,
"Of thy lost dreams and faith—thy Long Ago." . . .

To-day, awake in my dark world, I know
It was my Youth I saw—my Youth long dead,
Once in a dream.

DEAD LEAVES

O Swallow, when the dead leaves come
   Thou flee'st away.
This nest is cold, this tree is dumb,
And over all this sky is gray.
But life is all a joyous day
   Where thou art fled,
And thou forgettest that these leaves are dead.

So hearts have Autumn days, O Swallow,
   And leaves that die.
Could I but follow thee—but follow,
And reach that other warmer sky,
And thus be happy by-and-by
   In some new way!
But all my leaves are dead and I must stay.

My leaves are dead, and yet I cannot fly.

PEACE

God spoke to her, and so she fell asleep.
I laid a white fair lily on her heart,
And when I saw her face I could not weep.

It had the peace Death only understands;
And when I knew she would not wake on earth
I laid my heart between her folded hands.

God spoke to her so softly, saying: "Rest."
And when she wakes in heaven, she will find
My lily and my heart upon her breast.

TRANSLATIONS

DEDICATIONS

FROM HEINE

THE rare red rose loves the butterfly,
   Who drifts to her deep-belled heart;
The butterfly loves the golden sun,
   And flutters up to his dart.

Prithee, by whom is the rose beloved?
   I would I could know by whom.
Is it the sweet-voiced Nightingale
   Or the star of the dead Day's tomb?

I know not by whom is the rose beloved.
   My love is for near and far:
For Rose, and Sun, and Butterfly,
   And Nightingale, and Star.

ALL the stars, gold-footed, wander
  In the heavens still and bright;
Softly, that they need not waken
  Nature, in the arms of Night.

Rapt, attentive, stand the forests,
  Ev'ry leaf a small green ear;
And the dreamy hills are stretching
  Shadow-arms from far and near.

Hark!... what sound? A tender echo
  Stirs within my heart's deep vale.
Was it her loved voice, or was it
  But the hidden Nightingale?

I saw a small, white sea - gull,
  That fluttered up on high;
Way up from the dark waves' heaving
  The moon moved far in the sky.

The rocks with their brazen faces
  Rose up where the pale waves lie;
Now riseth, now sinketh, the sea - gull.
  The moon moved far in the sky.

O tender, fluttering Spirit,
  How sadly thy white wings lie!
Too near to thee is the water,
  Too far the moon in the sky.

SHADOW-KISSES, shadow-passion,
  Shadow-life, and all so strange.
Think'st thou, fool, in this world's fashion
  Things will last and never change?

All we love and have begotten
  Fade away, as dreams do creep;
And the heart, it is forgotten,
  And the eyes are closed in sleep.

As the moon's reflection trembleth,
  Where the wild, wide ocean waileth,
And herself most calm and placid,
  In the peaceful heaven traileth,

So thou wand'rest, my Belovèd,
  Far above me placid fleeting;
Only thy reflection trembleth
  In my own heart's troubled beating.

THE troubles crowd, and the bells are ringing,
　　And ah, my head is turned with madness:
The Spring-time and two sweet eyes gleaming
　　Have both conspired against my gladness.

The Spring-time and two sweet eyes gleaming
　　My heart in other paths have bidden.
I think the Nightingales and Roses
　　In this conspiracy are hidden.

SWEETLY float upon my heart,
　Little Bells loud-ringing;
Chime out tender Spring-tide songs,
　Towards the heavens springing.

Ring and race into the place
　Where the buds are sweeter.
When you close upon a rose,
　Tell her that I greet her.

.

My soul I will steep so softly
    In a lily's white, pure bell;
From the lily, swinging, ringing,
    A song of my Love will swell.

The song will float ever, undying,
    Like the kiss from her mouth's red flower,
She gave me once in that sweetest,
    That fleetest, dear, dead hour.

So you forget, and have forgotten all,
  That once for me alone your heart did beat;
Your little heart, so sweet and false and small,
  That nothing else could be more false or sweet.

So you forget the love and grief to-day,
  That in my heart, alas, were ever mate.
Which was the greater, love or sorrow? Nay,
  I know not, but I know that both were great.
20

I WANDER and weep in the forest;
   The throstle her tree-top doth keep.
She springeth and singeth so softly:
   "Ah, why dost thou wander and weep?"

The swallows, for they are thy sisters,
   Will answer thee better, I wis.
In a little brown nest they are living,
   Where my little love's window is.

In the golden Summer morning
　In the garden-path I come.
All the flowers sigh and whisper,
　But I wander sad and dumb.

All the flowers sigh and whisper,
　Bending to me in the sun:
" Be not angry with our sister,
　O thou sad and pallid One!"

In my life, so dark and dreary,
　　Once there came a golden ray;
But the tender light has faded,
　　And my sky is dark to-day.

When the children are in darkness,
　　Some kind heart will comfort bring,
And to chase their childish sorrow,
　　Some sweet voice a song will sing.

I, a foolish child, go singing,
　　In the darkness, in the rain;
Though my song may hardly please you,
　　Yet it frees me from my pain.

MEDITATION

[From Théophile Gautier]

O HEART's fair innocence so quickly fled away!
   Bright dreams where joy and love and happi-
    ness abide,
Illusions sweet that come but in the morn of day,
   Why do you never last until the even-tide?

Why? . . . As the hours speed, no dew-drop tears
   we find
   Most silvery and fresh upon the drooping flow-
    ers.
The frail anemone, unsheltered 'gainst the wind,
   Has lost its vivid glow before the ev'ning hours.

The stream is silver clear, and limpid at its birth,
   But in a little while its purity is gone.
A cloud across the sky that smiles serene on earth,
   And in a little while the dreary rain is born.

And thus the world is made. O Fate, supreme
    and sad !
As is the dream's dark shade, which ever swift
    appears,
What grieves us still remains—'tis fled what made
    us glad—
The rose lives but an hour—the cypress many
    years.

EPITAPH

[From Victor Hugo]

THE child was living to laugh and to play—
O Nature, why didst thou take him away?
Hast thou not thy birds as the rainbows bright?
Thy stars and thy woods, thy lakes and thy skies?
Why didst thou take from his mother's eyes,
And hide him, 'neath flowers away from sight?

No richer thou for this one child more,
Nor starlit Nature more glad than before.
And the mother's heart where such pain doth press,
Where each joy engenders a grief—the heart
Which is just as great as thou, Nature, art,
Is desolate for this one child less!

DEW-DROPS

[From Sully Prudhomme]

DREAMING I watch the silver limpid dew
Fall as in pearly drops on meadow-land,
Silv'ring the floweret - petals softest hue,
And scattered round by misty Night's cool hand.

Whence do they come, those trembling dew-drops
  pale?
No clouds appear to mar the sky's pure way.
Ere they were formed to fall in silver veil,
Within the bosom of the air they lay.

Whence come my tears? Across the twilight
  sky
The radiant hues fade soft and slow and
  bright. . . .
Deep in my soul those tears did hidden lie
Before they came to dim my eyes to - night.

Within each soul there lies a tenderness
   Touched by the bitterness of grief and fears ;
And oftentimes it is a mere caress
   That stirs and wakes to life these latent tears.

21

HERE BELOW

[From Sully Prudhomme]

Here below the lilacs soon are past,
And the birds' sweet chanting soon is o'er ;
I dream upon the Summer tides that last
        Evermore.

Here below Time's fading touch is cast
O'er the lips soft velvet bloom of yore.
I dream upon the kisses that do last
        Evermore.

Here below men's mourning tears fall fast
O'er the friendship days forever o'er.
I dream upon the friendships that do last
    -        Evermore.